THE RUSSIA-UKRAINE CONFLICT

A LEGAL DECONSTRUCTION OF RUSSIAN ACTS OF AGGRESSION

TEJAS SATEESHA HINDER

Acknowledgement

On completion of this work, I would like to thank my parents and family for supporting me in procuring the requisite secondary sources that I needed to undertake an exhaustive doctrinal approach.

I would like to thank my peers at the Cell for Human Unification and Development by Advancing Personalities for providing me with detailed insights on the issues that I analyse in this work.

I would like to finally express special gratitude to Ms. Arushi Bhagotra for standing as an emotional and motivating backbone amidst stressful situations created whenever multiple work commitments arose simultaneously in the course of finishing this book.

Launch of direct assault and violation of Ukrainian territorial sovereignty and integrity

Unlawaful intervention in affairs

The principle of non-intervention involves the right of every sovereign State to conduct its affairs without outside interference. The principle of non-intervention forbids all States to intervene directly or indirectly in the internal or external affairs of other States. This principle of customary international law has been recognized in UNGA Resolutions and judgements of this Court. The manner in which a government treats its own nationals in its territory is within its domestic jurisdiction. Intervention, even on moral grounds, has been held to be contrary to current international law.

Hence, in this instance, Ukraine has violated the principles of non-intervention as mentioned in the Resolutions of the UNGA, in the judgements of this court and by eminent jurists in the field of Public International Law.

The principle enshrined in Article 2(4) of the United Nations Charter ("UN Charter") has the character of international customary law. The Charter enshrines the principle of sovereign equality of all nations. The prohibited force under Article 2(4) of the Charter includes any kind of trans-border use of force, regardless of the intention of depriving the State of part of its territory. Hence in terms of its legal effect "sovereignty" implies "inviolability" prohibiting any kind of forcible cross-frontier activity. Ukraine, thus by sending its troops to Kudritan is guilty of violation of the principle of non-intervention.

Ukraine has acted in violation of the very basic purpose of the UN Charter, which is to maintain international peace and security and encourage peaceful means to settle international disputes.

There is no exception available for Ukraine to defend its violation of the principle of non-intervention. It cannot invoke the exception to self-defense or anticipatory self-defense due to the absence of armed attack and current present danger by Russia. The Charter recognizes self-defense under Article 51 and collective action pursuant to a Security Council resolution safeguarded by decision-making procedures that ensure a broad support in the world community under Chapter VII as exceptions to the well-established principle of non-intervention. The omission of explicit reference to humanitarian intervention must be assumed intentional. There is no basis in law for such an exception to Article 2(4).

The exception of self-defence is conditional upon an armed attack by the aggressor State. A State acting in self-defence acts in response to an imminent danger which must be serious, immediate and incapable of being countered by other means.

Further, there lies no case of anticipatory self-defense as the same does not exist in international law. Alternatively, even if the concept of anticipatory self-defense is presumed to exist, it has no application in the current dispute. The conditions underlying such an exception to the prohibition on use of force are- necessity, proportionality and immediacy. In order to fulfil these criteria, Ukraine needs to prove that there was no other means left except military recourse and that the intervention was done in response to a clear and present danger and not mere preparation.

United Nations Resolutions constitute 'subsequent practice' for interpreting United Nations Charter provisions. The Declaration states that "armed intervention and all other forms of interference or attempted threats against the personality of the State or against its political, economic and cultural elements are in violation of international law." In furtherance of this, it can be said that the ambush of the patrol, strikes on the Western airfields and subsequent attacks amount to armed intervention against the political elements of Russia, and the same is in violation of international law as under of the aforementioned provision.

The cases of the murdered Chinese in Indonesia, the war against Southern Sudanese, the events in Rwanda, Burundi, Kashmir, Naga and South Africa would have justified humanitarian intervention but states have not engaged themselves in the protection of the affected population and thus have reaffirmed the existing principle of non-intervention. Moreover, The Russian ambassador to the UN, in the start of the NATO campaign against Yugoslavia, said that the justification of attacks with the need for humanitarian intervention was completely untenable. In this instance, if there lies a claim by Ukraine that the intervention was necessary to prevent violence and violation of rights of people living in Kudritan due to acts of Russia or its Army, the same would not be justified in light of the aforementioned submission made.

Every state shall refrain from any action aimed at the partial or total disruption of the national unity and territorial integrity of any other state or country. In the Lotus Case, the court observed that the first and foremost restriction imposed by international law upon a state is that a state may not exercise its power in any form in the territory of another state. The Declaration on the Right to Development adopted by the General Assembly in Resolution 41/128 called in for states to take resolute action to eliminate "threats against national sovereignty, national unity and territorial integrity."

In the World Summit Outcome, 2005, the world leaders reaffirmed "to support all efforts to uphold the sovereign equality of all states, and respect their territorial integrity and political independence."

As per the Manila Declaration, all States shall refrain in their international relations from the threat or use of force against the territorial integrity or political independence of any State.

Constitution of an Internationally wrongful Act

Principle of Non–Intervention, derived from Customary International Law, is the intervention in the choice of a political, economic, social & cultural system, and the formulation of foreign policy through the methods of coercion, it is a violation of the international legal norm. One of the imperative elements of non-intervention principle is coercion. Coercion refers to an intervention which uses force, either in the direct form of military action, or in the indirect form of support for subversive or terrorist armed activities within another State. It includes indirect interference through economic, political, and diplomatic means which aims to impose a certain conduct of consequence on a sovereign State. Only those actions would be considered to be coercive that are intended to be coercive by intentionally instigating or aggravating civil unrest.

"Transboundary harm" means harm caused in the territory of or in other places under the jurisdiction or control of a State other than the State of origin, whether or not the States concerned share a common border. It has been stated that no state has the right to use or permit the use of its territory in such a manner as to cause injury to the territory of another or the properties or person therein. Under the duty to prevent trans-boundary harm, states must keep activities within their jurisdiction or control from causing damage to the environment and humans in other States or outside the boundaries of national jurisdiction. which is a recognized principle of customary international law. Trans-boundary harm recognizes - (i) Physical relationship between the activity concerned and the damage caused, (ii) Human Causation, (iii) Threshold of severity that calls for legal action, (iv) Transboundary movement of the harmful effects. Moreover, in the case of **Nicaragua v. Costa Rica** before the International Court of Justice, the court observed that States have an obligation under customary international law to exercise due diligence in preventing significant transboundary harm. Due diligence is an accepted standard for the duty to prevent transboundary harm. The test of due diligence requires reasonable efforts to take appropriate measures in a timely fashion, with States having discretion to take measures which are necessary, appropriate, and feasible. Due diligence is not a guarantee that harm will be prevented, but an obligation for a State to exert its best efforts to minimise risk.

In this instance, the attacks carried out by Russia on the territory of Ukraine violate (i) Article 2(4) of the Charter of the United Nations; (ii) the principle of non-intervention, as enshrined in The Charter of the United Nations and Resolution 2131 of The General Assembly of the United Nations, and as put forward by various opinions of judges of The International Court of Justice as well as eminent jurists in the field of Public International Law.

Article 2(4) requires that states refrain in their international relations, from the threat or use of force, "All Members shall refrain in their international relations from the threat or use of force against the territorial integrity or political independence of any state or in any manner inconsistent with the Purposes of the United Nations." It endows the prohibition of force as a general and authoritative principle. The substantial majority of legal scholars attribute the norm contained in Article 2(4) a jus cogens character. The same has also been regarded as jus cogens by the International Court of Justice and the International Law Commission.

Further, the Article is a strict prohibition; an incursion into the territory of another State constitutes an infringement of Article 2(4), even if it is not intended to deprive that State of part of its territory and if the invading troops are meant to withdraw immediately after completing a temporary and limited operation. In order for the force used against a State to be illegitimate, force has to be aimed towards the territorial integrity or political independence of said State. The standard of using forcible measures encompass sending undercover agents to kill an individual, therefore a covert military mission into another State satisfies the conditions of a forcible measure.

The bombings carried out by Russia on the territory of Ukraine on 6th November, 2018 constituted use of force under Article 2(4), and the same, by taking place over the territory of Ukraine, causing several causalities of civilians in addition to killing several militants, violated the sovereignty and territorial integrity of Ukraine, and was not consistent with the purposes of The Charter of The United Nations, hence violating Article 2(4) of The Charter of The United Nations Non-Intervention under customary international law imposes a duty on states to refrain from intervening, directly or indirectly, in the internal and external affairs within the domestic jurisdiction of any state. Domestic jurisdiction of a state is where state is the sole judge, with sovereign authority to decide freely. The manner in which a government treats its own nationals in its territory is within its domestic jurisdiction. Furthermore, in secessionist conflicts, the General Assembly and Security Council have upheld the sovereign authority of parent state within its territory.

The principle of non-intervention, as one of the fundamental norms of international law, is embodied in the Charter of the United Nations and firmly established in state practice and customary international law. Among early treaty formulations of the principle was Article 15(8) of the Covenant of the League of Nations and the Montevideo Convention on Rights and Duties of States of 1933, which prohibited "interference with the freedom, the sovereignty or other internal affairs, or the processes of the Governments of other nations," together with the Additional Protocol on Non-Intervention of 1936.

Resolution 2131 (XX) presents the United Nations General Assembly's Declaration on the Inadmissibility of Intervention in the Domestic Affairs of States and the Protection of their Independence and Sovereignty, in which the Assembly "solemnly declares" that "no state has the right to intervene, directly or indirectly, for any reason whatever, in the internal and external affairs of any other state". The declaration condemns "armed intervention and all other forms of interference or attempted threats against the personality of the state or against its political, economic and cultural elements". This principle is reiterated in almost the same wording in the section on "The principle concerning the duty not to intervene in matters within the domestic jurisdiction of any State" of the 1970 General Assembly Declaration on Principles of International Law concerning Friendly Relations and Co-operation among States in accordance with the Charter of the United Nations. This latter declaration not only condemns interventions, but also declares them to be a "violation of international law" and therefore subjects them to international liability. The jus cogens character of the principle of non-intervention is widely upheld by governments. The General Assembly, in its Declaration of 9 December 1981, made it clear that the non-intervention principle embodies the requirement that States "refrain from entering into agreements with other States with a view to intervening or interfering in internal or external affairs of other States". The general position of States that no agreement may be validly entered into in violation of the non-intervention principle strongly suggests that they regard this principle to be of a jus cogens character.

According to International Court of Justice, an intervention is prohibited by international law if:

a. It impinges on matters as to which each state is permitted to make decisions by itself freely;
b. It involves interference regarding this freedom by methods of coercion, especially force.

In 1966 the General Assembly of the United Nations resolved that, no state has the right to intervene, directly or indirectly, for any reason whatever in the internal or external affairs of any other state. Consequently, armed intervention and all other forms of interference or attempted threats against the personality of the state or against its political, economic, or cultural elements are condemned.

The principle of non- intervention has been given general recognition in the International Court of Justice case of Nicaragua, the principle of non-intervention involves the right of every sovereign State to conduct its affairs without outside interference; though examples of trespass against this principle are not infrequent, the Court considers that it is part and parcel of customary international law. As the Court has observed, "Between independent States, respect for territorial sovereignty is an essential foundation of international relations, and international law requires political integrity also to be respected. The existence in the opinio juris of States of the principle of non-intervention is backed by established and substantial practice. The non-intervention principle is a necessary derivative from the principle of state sovereignty. Every state is sovereign and equal in law vis-à-vis every other. Being equally sovereign, a state is not subject to any form of foreign interference in its own domestic matters except by consent. Therefore, no intervention, whether economic, political, military or otherwise, is tolerable without explicit prior agreements under international law. Armed intervention or other forms of intervention involving the use of force are further prohibited by the principle of non-use of force. Concerning the substance of the non-intervention principle, the International Court of Justice stated, "As regards the content of the principle of non-intervention, in view of the generally accepted formulations, the principle forbids all States or groups of States to intervene directly or indirectly in the internal or external affairs of other States. A prohibited intervention must accordingly be one bearing on matters in which each State is permitted, by the principle of State sovereignty, to decide freely.

The non-intervention principle is not only fundamental to the international legal system, but also peremptory in the sense that it cannot be modified or derogated from by the mere consent of two or more States in the form of a new practice or new treaty. Judge Sette Camara, in his separate concurring opinion in Nicaragua Case, correctly states that "the non-use of force as well as non-intervention – the latter as a corollary of the equality of States and self-determination – are not only cardinal principles of customary international law but could in addition be recognized as peremptory rules of customary international law which impose obligations on all States."

The attacks launched on the territory of Ukraine (part of Kudritan on which the attack was launched belonged to Ukraine) amounted intervention with and violation of the sovereignty of Ukraine, as it amounted to armed interference against the political and economic will of the State (Ukraine), disrupted elements of the same in addition to disrupting the existing state of affairs and involved interference with regard to the freedom granted to it under the Statute of The International Court of Justice by methods of coercion, especially force. Hence, the act amounts to a violation of the principle of non-intervention as enshrined in The Charter of the United Nations and Resolution 2131 of The General Assembly of the United Nations, and as put forward by various opinions of judges of The International Court of Justice as well as eminent jurists in the field of Public International Law. An internationally wrongful act constitutes State responsibility, coupled with a breach of an international obligation.

There is a breach of an international obligation by a State when the act of that State is not in conformity with what is required of it by that obligation. Hence, by breaching the responsibility imposed on it by the Charter of The United Nations, Resolutions of The United Nations General Assembly and principles set forth by The International Court of Justice, there has been an internationally wrongful act committed by The Republic of Ukraine.

Non-justifiability under International Law

The attacks over the territory of Ukraine carried out by Russia were neither a valid exercise of self-defence, nor were it a justifiable counter-measure. Hence, as (i) the attacks were not a valid exercise of self-defence and (ii) were not valid and justifiable countermeasures, they cannot be justified under international law.

Not a valid exercise of self-defence

The International Court of Justice, in the Nicaragua case, placing reliance on Article 3(g) of the 1974 Resolution on the Definition of Aggression laid down that the definition of 'armed attack' as has been mentioned in the Charter could extend to cover attacks by 'armed bands, groups, irregulars or mercenaries', however these actors must have been sent 'by or on behalf of a state'.

Further, the International Court of Justice in its advisory opinion on the Legal Consequences of the Construction of a Wall in the Occupied Palestinian Territory held that the right of self-defence can only be invoked in response to an armed attack 'by one state against another state'. Therefore, the provision for taking measure for self - defence as per Article 51 of the Charter of The United Nations cannot be exercised in the present fact situation as there was no evidence which highlighted the fact that the Russia was under a threat of attack by Ukraine.

Such interpretations of Article 51 of The Charter of The United Nations and the subsequent modification of customary international law to allow the right of self-defence against non-state actors. In the Asylum case, the International Court of Justice suggested that for a customary rule to be accepted there must be a constant and uniform usage of the same. In the 2613th meeting of the United Nations Security Council, the representative of Greece and Madagascar propounded the fact that acts of terrorism were not enough grounds for a government to launch armed attacks on a third country.

Further, in the aftermath of a military operation in self - defence by the Colombian armed force targeting a Colombian Revolutionary Armed Forces training camp situated close to the Colombian - Ecuadorian border, which resulted in the incursion by the Colombian armed forces into Ecuadorian territory, the governments of Ecuador and Venezuela condemned the same and halted diplomatic ties with the nation of Colombia and subsequently, the Organization of American States (OAS), proclaimed that the Colombian incursion in self-defence, 'was a violation of the sovereignty and territorial integrity of Ecuador and the principles of international law.

In light of the evidence of state practice presented above, which leans towards and away from accepting the legality of the exercise of the right of self - defence guaranteed by Article 51 of the Charter of The United Nations, it can be clearly interpreted that the necessary condition of constant and uniform usage of a customary rule for the same to be accepted has not been fulfilled. Instant customary laws cannot be evolved in this matter as the same matter concerns the principles of sovereignty and territorial integrity of nations, which is a right guaranteed to all nations across the world by virtue of the Charter.

Even a small amount of state practice can result in the creation of a rule for the same however this depends on the nature of the rule in question. Given the fact that the rule in question in the present situation is that of right of self-defence against non-state actors operating in third-party countries and by logical extension the violation of the territorial integrity of a nation, a certain amount of state practice in favour of allowing for the exercising of such a right cannot be interpreted as a new customary rule with regard to the same and as has been stated earlier, uniform and constant usage of such a practice has to be in existence for such a rule to be formulated.

Hence, the alleged right of self-defence that the State of Russia cannot be justified on the basis of Customary International Law due to the insufficiency of the amount of state practice in order to aid in the formulation of a customary rule to support their incursions into the territories of the Russia, which has resulted in the violation of the territorial integrity and the sovereignty of the nation.

The International Court of Justice and Scholars in the field of International Law have found that non-state actors cannot commit 'armed attacks' under Article 51 of The Charter of The United Nations; thus, they may be targeted without the territorial State's consent only if their actions are attributable to that State. Even if an exception exists for self-defence within States 'unable or unwilling' to prevent armed attacks, that test is not met here. Thus, self-defence has not been rightfully exercised by Russia.

The rule of self-defence has also been enshrined in Article 21 of The Articles on the Responsibility of States for Internationally Wrongful Acts, which specifies that this rule finds application only in cases where the act being defended against was performed by an attacking state which in this matter is not the case, so self-defence would not be applicable in this instance.

Should the Court at any point find that Russia exercised legitimate self-defence, the principles of necessity and proportionality were not followed. As part of customary international law, self-defence has to satisfy the condition of necessity. Necessity is interpreted as self-defence being the last resort after all peaceful measures have failed.

Article 33(1) of the Charter of the United Nations puts forward a duty to seek for peaceful means to settle a dispute, e.g. by a negotiation or by resorting to a regional agency. If a State were able to achieve the same result by measures not involving the use of armed force, it would have no justification for adopting conduct which contravenes the general prohibition against the use of armed force.

In this instance, no attempt was made by Russia to settle the dispute by peaceful means, be it either through an effort to open a peaceful dialogue or even exertion of diplomatic pressure over Ukraine. Hence, the test of necessity is not satisfied, and thus Russia's claim of exercise of self-defence is not justified.

Not justifiable as a countermeasure

Countermeasures that violate fundamental human rights obligations and involve the use or threat of force are unlawful. Countermeasures must be necessary "to safeguard an essential interest against a grave and imminent peril" and proportionate, including quantitatively equivalent, in response to an internationally wrongful act.

In this instance, since the attacks carried out by Russia over Ukraine caused the death of innocent civilians, thus violating their human rights as granted to them under The Four Geneva Conventions and The Additional Protocol I of 1997. Therefore, the conduct of attacks is not justified as a counter-measure, and hence, self-defence cannot be rightfully claimed by Russia.

Hence, there being a violation of sovereignty and territorial integrity of Ukraine by Russia's attacks on its territory, and the same being unjustified on grounds of self-defence as well as that of a countermeasure, Russia's attacks on the territory of Ukraine are in violation of sovereignty and territorial integrity of Ukraine and amounted to the violation of the provisions of The United Nations Charter on the use of force and other relevant international law.

Violation of Customary International Law by clandestine support of combatants

In the same regard, Article 1(3) of the Convention provides that states should forbid in supplying arms or war materials with the only exception, i.e. it is allowed when meant for the government. So it can be very well deduced that assistance to the incumbent government is permissible, not to the insurgent group.

The Security Council resolution clearly states that states should not provide any form of support to acts causing widespread panic and prevent people from planning or facilitating such attacks.

United Nations Resolutions constitute 'subsequent practice' for interpreting United Nations Charter provisions. The Declaration states that 'armed intervention' and all other forms of interference or attempted threats against the personality of the State or against its political, economic and cultural elements are in violation of international law.

The aiding of militants, which led to multiple incidents of armed attack, was an indirect armed intervention by Ukraine, thus violating UNGA Resolution 2625.

The resolution reflects the customary law and makes a clear statement for states to strictly observe the principle of non-intervention to ensure peaceful coexistence and provides with an obligation not to support or promote any armed activities against another state. Para 1 and Para 3 of the resolution are relevant in this regard.

Clause four of the aforementioned resolution urgently calls for international cooperation to prevent and eradicate acts of terrorism, and stresses that those responsible for aiding, supporting, or harbouring the perpetrators, organizers and sponsors of such acts will be held accountable.

According to Article 4(g) of the aforementioned resolution, The sending by or on behalf of a State of armed bands, groups, irregulars or mercenaries, which carry out acts of armed force against another State of such gravity as to amount to the acts listed above, or its substantial involvement therein, amounts to an act of aggression, and Article 5 of the aforementioned resolution states that no justification for any reason, be it political, economic or social, can justify the act of aggression. Therefore, in this instance the act of Ukraine is violative of International Law as under Resolution 3314 of the UNGA and cannot be justified.

Rougier's 'Le Théorie de l'Intervention d'Humanité' in his work, rejected the idea of unilateral intervention. It is to be understood that states would rarely intervene unless they would derive benefits from such an intervention, otherwise the political cost would be very high.61 Moreover, in the Corfu Channel case, The Court noted that 'respect for territorial sovereignty is an essential foundation of international relations'. No state may organize, assist, foment, finance, incite or tolerate subversive, terrorist or armed activities directed towards the violent overthrow of regime of another state, or interfere in civil strife in another state. The principle of effective control has been recognized by the same court in cases such as Nicaragua Case and **Bosnia and Herzegovina v. Serbia and Montenegro** where the Court relied on the Effective Control test.

As far as intervention is concerned, "When a foreign state recognizes a state of insurgency, it merely acknowledges the fact of the insurrection, but does not create any new international status between it and the parties to the strife." The states are barred from providing direct assistance to such groups, the right to provide assistance as a non-neutral pertained only to aiding the incumbent government.

Violation of Human Rights

Imposition of violence and failure to demarcate between civilians and combatants

The International Criminal Tribunal for the former Yugoslavia (ICTY) proposed a general definition of international armed conflict. In the

Tadic case, the Tribunal stated that "an armed conflict exists whenever there is a resort to armed force between States". This definition has been adopted by other international bodies since then.

According to D. Schindler, "the existence of an armed conflict within the meaning of Article 2 common to the Geneva Conventions can always be assumed when parts of the armed forces of two States clash with each other."

An armed conflict arises whenever there is fighting between States or protracted armed violence between government authorities and organized armed groups or just between organized armed groups.

Common Article 2 to the Geneva Conventions of 1949 states that, in addition to the provisions which shall be implemented in peacetime, the present Convention shall apply to all cases of declared war or of any other armed conflict which may arise between two or more of the High Contracting Parties, even if the state of war is not recognized by one of them. The Convention shall also apply to all cases of partial or total occupation of the territory of a High Contracting Party, even if the said occupation meets with no armed resistance. The Commentary of the Geneva Conventions of 1949 confirms that any difference arising between two States and leading to the intervention of armed forces is an armed conflict within the meaning of Article 2, even if one of the Parties denies the existence of a state of war. It makes no difference how long the conflict lasts, or how much slaughter takes place.

According to D. Schindler, "Any kind of use of arms between two States brings the Geneva Conventions into effect." H.P. Gasser explains that "any use of armed force by one State against the territory of another, triggers the applicability of the Geneva

Conventions between the two States. It is also of no concern whether or not the party attacked resists. As soon as the armed forces of one State find themselves with wounded or surrendering members of the armed forces or civilians of another State on their hands, as soon as they detain prisoners or have actual control over a part of the territory of the enemy State, then they must comply with the relevant convention."

Since there exists an armed conflict in this instance, it attracts the provisions of the Geneva Conventions and the Additional Protocols, and there arises an obligation for Russia and Ukraine to comply with the same.

It is to be noted that the attacks carried out by Russia on Ukraine caused civilian casualties and as per the Convention and humanitarian on the civilians prohibited. Article 50(1) of Additional protocol defines that the population is a civilian under the meaning of International Law. The influx of the Russian Army in Ukraine in an attempt to prevent the separatist movement led to severe violation of rights of the demonstrators as there were several casualties of innocent civilians in addition to the demonstrators that were caused.

Article 48 of the Additional Protocol lays an obligation on the parties to the conflict to distinguish between civilians and combatants. In the **Nuclear Weapons case**, the International Court of Justice in the advisory opinion confirmed that the principle of distinction holds that States must not make civilians the object of attack.

The Security Council laid emphasis on the protection of civilians in armed conflict where it reaffirmed the principle of distinction as being applicable to all armed conflicts. It is noted that in pursuance of such military actions, Russia killed many civilians.

Resolution (2675 XXV) states that in conduct of the military operations during armed conflict distinction must be made between civilians and the combatants and hence not be made subject to military operations.

Article 52(1) prohibits the attack on civilian objects and specifically stipulates that civilians should not be an object of attack. The United Nations Security Council has repeatedly condemned the failure to ensure that civilians are not made subject to attack, either deliberately or through negligence, in conflicts such as Rwanda, Burundi and Sierra Leone.

Article 51(1), Article 51(2) and Article 51(3) of the Additional Protocol I contain provisions related to the protection of the civilians during armed conflict. In the case of **Prosecutor v. Stanislav Galic** the ICTY held that in case of armed conflict attacks should not be directed towards the civilians.

Article 13(2) of the part IV of Additional Protocol II to the Geneva Convention of 1949 states that civilian population shall not be the object of attack and acts or threats of violence.

Article 13(3) states that this protection shall be enjoyed by all civilians who have no part to play in the hostilities. By launching attacks on the territory of Ukraine, having the knowledge that the same may cause civilian casualties, causing the same, Russia made civilians the subject of the attack, thus violating Articles 51(1), 51(2), 51(3) and 52(1) of the Additional Protocol I.

The right to life has been recognized as a norm of jus cogens and is therefore binding upon all States, whether or not they are parties to the treaties that contain such prohibition. Thus, it prescribes that

States have a peremptory obligation90 to ensure the preservation of the right to life and prohibition of torture.
Article 75 of the additional protocol gives fundamental guarantee to the civilians during an armed conflict. Article 75(2)(a) and Article 75(2)(e) prohibits any kind of violent act at any time and any place whatsoever against the civilians. It can be very well deduced from the facts that the attacks, the acts of violence were committed against the civilians by the forces of Russia.

The International Covenant on Civil and Political Rights ("ICCPR") provides that the right to life is an inherent right and no person may be deprived of it arbitrarily. This right is defined by the Human Rights Committee as the 'supreme right'. The aforementioned provisions, by virtue of causing civilian casualties by air strikes and the Russian Army's infliction of harm during its influx, have been violated by Russia. Russia has also violated the Rule 1 of the customary international humanitarian law which prohibits any attack on the civilians by the parties to the conflict. In the **Kassem case**, Israel's military court at Ramallah recognized the immunity of civilians from direct attacks as one of the basic rules of international humanitarian law

The people of Ukraine are provided protection under the Geneva Convention relative to the protection of civilian persons in time of war (IV Convention).96 Protocol additional to the Geneva Conventions of August 12, 1949, and relating to the protection of victims of international armed conflicts prohibits violence to the life, health and physical or mental well-being of persons, in particular murder as well as cruel treatment such as torture, mutilation or any form of corporal punishment are prohibited. Human rights of the civilians were violated by the carrying out of attacks as well as civilian casualties during the influx of the Russian Army.

Prevention from holding a plebiscite: Denial of Right to Self-Determination

Self-determination has the status of jus cogens and an erga omnes obligation. The peoples' right to self-determination is an inalienable right of erga omnes character.

Erga omnes are obligations owed to the international community as a whole. Thus, all States have an obligation to promote the realisation of the right to self-determination. There existed an obligation on Russia to realize and recognize the right to self-determination of the people of Ukraine, which it failed to do.

Declaration of Friendly Relations 1970 set out internationally agreed basic principles of international law, that subjection of peoples to alien subjugation, domination and exploitation constitutes a violation of the principle of equal rights and self-determination of peoples, as well as a denial of fundamental human rights, and is contrary to the Charter of United Nations. Under the principle of self- determination, a group with common identity and link to a defined territory is allowed to decide its political future in a democratic fashion. A people can be said to have realised its right to self-determination when they have either (1) established a sovereign and independent state; (2) freely associated with another state or (3) integrated with another state after freely having expressed their will to do so.

In this instance, there was a plebiscite to be held in order to democratically determine whether the people of Ukraine wanted to accede to Russia, and the same was necessary to determine its political future. By not holding the plebiscite, there was never an opportunity given to the people of Ukraine to choose the State they wanted to accede to, and hence were denied their right to self-determination.

Right to self-determination, recognised in the UN Charter, Declaration of Friendly Relations 1970, International Covenant on Civil and Political Rights 1996 and the International Covenant on Economic, Social and Cultural Rights 1966, is a rule of international law as seen by United Nations declarations and resolutions, and actual state practice in the process of decolonization.

Common Article 1 in the International Covenant on Civil and Political Rights and the International Covenant on Economic, Social and Cultural Rights define the right of self-determination as, "All peoples have the right of self-determination. By virtue of that right they freely determine their political status and freely pursue their economic, social and cultural development."

It gives right of self-determination to the people of a country. A "people" can be said to have realised its right to self-determination when they have either (1) established a sovereign and independent state; (2) freely associated with another state or (3) integrated with another state after freely having expressed their will to do so. Thus, having satisfied the aforementioned criteria, the people of Ukraine qualify as people, and have their right to self-determination is protected.

The right to self-determination is the right to decide on the political status of a people and its place in the international community in relation to other states. The consistent state practice in conformity with the UN resolutions formed the international customary rules on the external self-determination of colonial peoples and peoples under foreign military occupation. The United Nations Millennium Declaration upholds the right to self-determination of peoples under colonial domination and foreign occupation.

Article 21(3) of the Universal Declaration of Human Rights states that, "the will of the people shall be the basis of authority of the government." Thus, by denying the people of Ukraine the right to self-determination, Russia has violated ICCPR, ICESCR, UN Charter and UDHR.

The holding of a plebiscite in order to establish the will of the people with respect to a change of status and other matters is a widely accepted act of self-determination and is widely supported by state practice. Freedom of a plebiscite requires the absence or at least restraint of military forces of the opposing parties and a neutrality of public authorities.

The Code of Good Practice on Referendums also provides for a number of general procedural requirements. The code requires the existence of a referendum law that regulates the procedure of the vote, and customary international law demands the presence of domestic and international observers. The application of the right of self-determination requires a free and genuine expression of the will of the peoples concerned. The importance of a plebiscite in the exercise of the right of self-determination has been recognised and it has been said that the issue of independence is possibly the most important decision that a political community may take by democratic means and hence, the matter requires the broadest possible commitment of the citizens to the resolution of the issue.

Indiscriminate use of Biological and Chemical Weapons

Article 1 of the Comprehensive Nuclear Test Ban Treaty ("CTBT") directs states to not carry out any nuclear weapon test explosion or any other nuclear explosion, and to prohibit and prevent any such nuclear explosion at any place under its jurisdiction or control. Therefore, in this instance, if Russia attempt to fire missiles, it violates Article 1 of the CTBT.

Article 2(5) of the CTBT directs state parties to cooperate with the Organization in the exercise of its functions in accordance with this Treaty and consult, directly among themselves, or through the Organization or other appropriate international procedures, including procedures within the framework of the United Nations and in accordance with its Charter, on any matter which may be raised relating to the object and purpose, or the implementation of the provisions, of this Treaty. Therefore, there existed an obligation on Ukraine to co-operate with organizations in accordance with the framework of the UN and avoid the testing of nuclear weapons. Hence, Ukraine, by testing and test-firing nuclear devices and missiles, respectively, has violated this Article.

Under Article 3(1)(a), Russia was under an obligation to prohibit natural and legal persons anywhere on its territory or in any other place under its jurisdiction as recognized by international law from undertaking any activity prohibited to a State Party under this Treaty. By its very governmental institution testing nuclear devices and arsenals, Russia would fail in its obligation to prevent agencies from testing nuclear devices and missiles if it fires any.

The Biological Weapons Convention prohibits the development of biological agents or toxins, as well as of weapons, equipment or means of delivery designed to use such agents or toxins for hostile purposes or in armed conflict Further, Article 1 clarifies that the prohibition on biological agents and toxins is not absolute; it only applies to such activities that have no justification for prophylactic, protective or other peaceful purposes. It is not the object itself, but the purpose of its usage that is prohibited.

The Biological Weapons Conventions ("BWC") imposes an obligation of due diligence as an obligation to prevent the development or production biological agents, toxins, weapons or of the equipment. Due diligence is an accepted standard for the duty to prevent harm, and States are not automatically liable for damage caused. The test requires reasonable efforts to take appropriate measures in a timely fashion, with States having discretion to take measures which are necessary, appropriate, and feasible. The duty of due diligence is an obligation of conduct, not an obligation of result and States are considered to have fulfilled their duty when due diligence is exercised, whether or not harm has already occurred.

Article 10 of the BWC stipulates that State Parties shall undertake to facilitate, and have the right to participate in, the fullest possible exchange of scientific and technological information for the use of biological agents and toxins for peaceful purposes. Further, it states that the convention shall avoid hampering the economic or technological development of State Parties in the field of peaceful biological activities.

The right of all the States to develop and use scientific research and discoveries exclusively for peaceful purposes without any discrimination has been considered an inalienable right by the United Nations General Assembly. Further, this Court held in the **Whaling case** that programmes otherwise prohibited through treaties that are only allowed for purposes of scientific research should be supported, as long as the scientific purposes are peaceful.

Stoppage of flow of water and the detriment to Human Rights

Shared water resources are governed by the principle of equitable use in customary international law. States share a "community of interest" in these resources.

Article 2 of the Helsinki Rules defines an international drainage basin as "an international drainage basin is a geographical area extending over two or more States determined by the watershed limits of the System of waters, including surface and underground waters, flowing into a common terminus." It can be inferred from the definition that the Sindhu River constitutes an international drainage basin.

Article IV of The Helsinki Rules states that Basin States are entitled to a reasonable and equitable share in the beneficial uses of the waters of an international drainage basin. In light of this Article, Ukraine was entitled to its reasonable and equitable share in the Sindhu River by virtue of being a basin state in reference to the Sindhu River.

Economic and social needs of each Basin State, the population dependent on the waters of the basin in each basin State, the comparative costs of alternative means of satisfying the economic and social needs of each basin State and the degree to which the needs of a basin State may be satisfied and without causing substantial injury to a co-basin State, are relevant factors in determining reasonable and equitable share of international drainage basin. In this instance, if these factors are looked upon, it can be inferred that the blocking the Sindhu River was not justified as, it was a source to meet social needs for the people of Ukraine and the population of Ukraine was dependent on it to meet its needs. Further, the blockade would lead to substantial injury of the people of Ukraine who were dependent on it to meet their needs, and hence, injure a co-basin state. Therefore, the blockade would violate Article V of The Helsinki Rules.

In the United States, in the earliest of the river water cases (**Kansas v. Colorado**), the Supreme Court held that the dispute over sharing of water resources must be settled on the basis of equality of rights.

In other cases, the Supreme Court has applied in interstate water disputes the doctrine of equitable apportionment. In India, in a dispute between Sind and the Punjab, concerning the use of the waters of the Indus system, the Report of the Indus Commission of 1941 (Rao Commission Report) upheld the rule relating to equitable apportionment. In the River Krishna dispute, the tribunal, constituted by the Central Government to settle the dispute between the states of Maharashtra, Karnataka and Andhra Pradesh, decided that groundwater is a relevant factor to be taken into consideration for equitable distribution of water. In the Narmada dispute, again, between the states of Madhya Pradesh, Maharashtra and Gujarat, the tribunal decided on the basis of the principle of equitable apportionment.

In the judgement of the German Staatsgerichtsh of in the **Donauversinkung Case**, the principle of equitable apportionment of water was applied. In a dispute between the cantons of Zurich and Aargau, the Federal Court (Bundesgericht) of Switzerland affirmed the equal rights of the cantons to use the public watercourses.

The Italian Court of Cassation in **Société Energie Electrique v. Compagnia Imprese Elettriche Liguri**, affirmed the principle of a community of ownership of water resources. In the case of **Württemberg v. Baden**, the Supreme Court of Germany grounded its decision on the principle of equitable utilization.

In other cases, the Supreme Court has applied in interstate water disputes the doctrine of equitable apportionment. In India, in a dispute between Sind and the Punjab, concerning the use of the waters of the Indus system, the Report of the Indus Commission of 1941 (Rao Commission Report) upheld the rule relating to equitable apportionment. In the River Krishna dispute, the tribunal, constituted by the Central Government to settle the dispute between the states of Maharashtra, Karnataka and Andhra Pradesh, decided that groundwater is a relevant factor to be taken into consideration for equitable distribution of water. In the Narmada dispute, again, between the states of Madhya Pradesh, Maharashtra and Gujarat, the tribunal decided on the basis of the principle of equitable apportionment.

The Law acknowledges that the obligation to equitably use a transboundary water resource would not apply in case of an emergency situation. However, for an emergency to exist, an event must cause, or pose an imminent threat of causing, "serious harm", which must be more than mere "significant harm".

The right to permanent sovereignty over natural wealth and resources is a rule of customary international law that requires its exercise through the mutual respect of states based on their sovereign equality. Since flowing water respects no national borders, transboundary freshwater systems, which largely concern aquifers, fall into the realm of international water law and not within the purview of a single state's sovereign rights.

It has been mentioned in Russia-Ukraine Water Agreement that each side shall receive unrestricted use all those waters of the Western Rivers which India is under obligation to let flow and that Russia shall be under an obligation to let flow all the waters of the Western Rivers, and shall not permit any interference with these waters.

In this instance, by blocking the supply of the water of the Sindhu River, the civilians, who were not a party to conflict, and were dependent on the water of the Sindhu River, were treated as targets in the conflict. Article 52(1) prohibits the attack on civilian objects and specifically stipulates that civilians should not be an object of attack. The United Nations Security Council has repeatedly condemned the failure to ensure that civilians are not made subject to attack, either deliberately or through negligence, in conflicts such as Rwanda, Burundi and Sierra Leone.

Russia violated Article 6 of the covenant as it confers the right to life. This is the very basic Human Rights conferred on every individual by law. Also, Russia has violated the Rule 1 of the customary international humanitarian law which prohibits any attack on the civilians by the parties to the conflict.

Contents

Printed by Libri Plureos GmbH in Hamburg, Germany